MW01102310

Especially for

Clara & Dan

From

Jessica & Michael

Date

July 26, 2014

ISBN 978-1-60260-820-7

Text without credits taken from *Daily Wisdom for Couples* by Toni Sortor and Pamela McQuade, published by Barbour Publishing, Inc.

Published by Barbour Publishing, Inc., P.O. Box 719, Uhrichsville, Ohio 44683, www.barbourbooks.com

Our mission is to publish and distribute inspirational products offering exceptional value and biblical encouragement to the masses.

Member of the
Evangelical Christian
Publishers Association

Printed in China.

Moments of Connection for Couples

BARBOUR
PUBLISHING

Part of God's Plan

Then the Lord God said, "It is not good that the man should be alone; I will make him a helper as his partner."

GENESIS 2:18 NRSV

Day 2

Shoring Up

Even happy marriages need work, and today is the best day to decide what part of your relationship could use some shoring up. Sit down with your spouse and compare notes on the strengths and weaknesses of your marriage. Confess any faults you may have noticed about yourself. Most importantly, pray that God will bless you with your best year yet.

GALE HYATT

Out of Love

Learning to work as a team and to trust our other "team member" takes time. As the years go by, we become more attuned to our partner. We discover what bugs them and what doesn't, and out of love—not fear—we adjust our actions. In time, there will be no fear between us, only patience and understanding.

Day 4

Loving Comfort

Oh, the comfort—the inexpressible comfort of feeling safe with a person—having neither to weigh thoughts nor measure words, but pouring them all right out, just as they are, chaff and grain together; certain that a faithful hand will take and sift them, keep what is worth keeping, and then with the breath of kindness blow the rest away.

DINAH MARIA MULOCK CRAIK

Day 5

Just the Two of You

Remember, not every activity requires a goal, and not all of our leisure time should be productive. What about just getting out of the house to admire God's world and spend some time with the one you love? Hold hands, bump shoulders, giggle a lot, and talk about your hopes and dreams. Just the two of you.

Day 6

Agree to Disagree

You're not perfect. . .and sometimes you and your spouse will disagree. When, after a few minutes of discussion, it becomes obvious that neither of you is going to change the other's mind, you both have to back off and agree to disagree.

Day 7

Better Off Unsaid

God knows every wrong you have ever committed, confessed, or hidden. If your conscience is burdened, ask Him for guidance on what you need to reveal. Trust Him to indicate what needs to be shared and what would be better off unsaid.

Day 8

Welcome Change

Father, we see each other changing as our relationship progresses and are uncertain how the changes will work out. Sometimes this frightens us. Give us the courage we need to welcome change and adapt to it so we will both be free to become the people You mean us to be.

Yesterday, Today, and Forever

People change as they go through life, sometimes for the better and sometimes not. A person—or a marriage—who does not grow or change is in trouble. Don't let change frighten you. As you age, change usually leads to a better life for you both. Only Jesus is the same yesterday, today, and forever.

Day 10

Eternal Gifts

When we meditate on eternal blessings, our momentary struggles are put in proper perspective. Earthly trials are temporary. Spiritual blessings are forever. Let's embrace the eternal gifts we have been given and praise God for His abundant provision!

JULIE RAYBURN

Answered Prayer

When our prayers are answered, what do we do? We give thanks in private, because whose business is it what we have prayed for and received? But Jesus says prayers are answered for only one reason: so that His actions on our behalf will bring glory to the Father. Do we give God the glory when our prayers are answered, or do we keep it to ourselves?

Home Improvement

Working together on a project will be worth a few laughs and a joint sense of accomplishment, even if a professional could have done the job better. You may not be qualified to start knocking down walls, but with a little advice from your home improvement center, you can learn to stop that annoying dripping faucet, change the faceplate on an outlet, or paint a dingy room.

Joined for Life

What greater thing is there for two human souls than to feel that they are joined for life—to strengthen each other in all labor, to rest on each other in all sorrow, to minister to each other in all pain, to be one with each other in silent, unspeakable memories.

GEORGE ELIOT

Day 14

The One You Love

Do you pray as regularly for your spouse as you once did for your parents and other family members? Your world is certainly more complex, as are your prayers, but taking time to ask God to bless the one you love might be the most important thing you can do for your marriage.

Strength to Make Peace

Father, we share so much as a couple that it's foolish to let a disagreement ruin the whole day. When we are arguing, remind us how much we love each other and give us the strength to make peace.

Day 16

Love Letter

If we want to show [God] how much we love Him and desire to understand His heart, we need to read His words. The Bible is our love letter from God, from the one true lover of our souls. Read it; wear it out!

LAURA FREUDIG

In God's Footsteps

Rather than remaking your spouse in your image of what he or she should be, follow in God's footsteps, offering mercy that encourages spiritual growth and maturity. Let compassion replace the judgment and condemnation. Soon you'll find yourself with an appreciative spouse, and not one who can't wait to pick out your flaws.

Day 18

The "Perfect" Marriage

Instead of making our spouses suffer for our selfishness, we should become increasingly sensitive to our mates. When we wrong each other, we ought to ask for and offer forgiveness as quickly as possible. . . . Can you imagine a more "perfect" marriage than being wed to a spouse like that?

Unconditionally

Help us love each other unconditionally, Lord, as You have loved us. We want to focus on the strengths You've given each of us and overcome the flaws.

100 Percent Joy

If you expect to give 100 percent, you will feel blessed when you see your spouse responding and giving to you—blessed because you didn't expect it. Disappointment, resentment, anger, and self-righteousness in your marriage will fade away as joy takes their place.

NICOLE O'DELL

A Successful Marriage

A successful marriage requires falling in love many times, always with the same person.

MIGNON MCLAUGHLIN

Day 22

All Things

He who did not spare His own Son, but delivered Him up for us all, how shall He not with Him also freely give us all things?

ROMANS 8:32 NKJV

Giving

To have a happy marital relationship means giving: time, effort, forgiveness, and that special every-morning kiss. It also means occasionally giving physical gifts: a how-to video he's wanted for a long time or a rose to tell her she's special. Whether it's a helping hand or a wrapped-up package, each gift shows your spouse you know what he or she needs and that you care for that need.

Day 24

Show Your Love

How do you show your love? How does your mate like to be shown love? Are the two the same? Take turns talking about the things you like that your mate does for you and the ways your husband or wife could improve. What "gifts" of time and consideration do you each need? What physical gifts make you the happiest?

Uninterrupted

Married couples need time together, uninterrupted by children, work, or family chores. Whether it's regular date nights or a few hours set aside for morning devotions and talk, schedule time to share. Your spouse will be pleased to no end.

Day 26

His Word

In our own lives, we experience new responsibilities, change, and fear of the unknown. Whether it is a promotion at work, a new baby, a cross-country move, or simply learning to love our spouses better, we experience our fair share of fear and discouragement. Be strong and courageous! Don't be afraid or discouraged! God promises to be with us wherever we go, and we can certainly trust Him to keep His word.

MANDY NYDEGGER

Even the Small Stuff

Lord God, we don't want a loveless marriage that gives no testimony to You. We want to keep the troubles in our relationship small by coming to You with even the small sins.

DAY 28

All Our Prayers

God loves to hear all our prayers, even the ones that begin "Help, quick!" When we see an out-of-control SUV hurtling down the road toward us, when we enter a crowded emergency room with a seriously ill loved one, or when we just don't know what to say in response to someone's critical words, God is only a prayer away.

God's Plan

Don't second-guess your decision to marry. Remember your marriage vows. You promised God that you would stay with this person for a lifetime, not until you tired of marriage or came to the sudden discovery that you didn't marry a "perfect" someone. Marriage isn't about your perfection or your spouse's; it's a covenant based on God's perfection and His plan for both of you.

Day 30

In His Hands

When we feel hopeless, and when our struggles overwhelm us, God is there. God loves us and wants to see us through our challenges. We simply must trust Him, placing our faith entirely in His hands, and believe that He will see us through.

MANDY NYDEGGER

Falling in Love

Don't let the media convince you that there is something missing in your partner because she's a little overweight or he is developing a bald spot on the top of his head. On those days when your spouse is obviously less than perfect, remember why you fell in love in the first place.

Day 32

A Lifetime

Father, neither of us is perfect by today's standards. But it was Your standards that attracted us to each other and will keep us together for the rest of our lives.

Young and Happy

Don't let all the issues and the children and the stress destroy the joy that comes with marriage. Never be too busy to enjoy quiet times with your spouse, to laugh or play like the children you once were together. Keep your relationship young and happy.

Day 34

Contentment

The Bible does not say you should refrain from wanting a better life for yourself. What God's Word does say is that until you achieve your desires, you should be content with what you have and not waste time envying others. You can sit in front of the TV all day, coveting the newest and the best, or you can get out there and earn what you want.

Teamwork

In spiritual matters, two individuals with differing talents but one faith can accomplish much for the church. One may be a fearless witness, while the other is an effective prayer warrior. One loves to teach Sunday school, while the other is a bear in the thrift shop. Whatever you do in life, do it as a team made up of two different people. Watch your accomplishments pile up, your fears blow away, and your joy abound.

Day 36

Worship Today

We tend to think of worship as an institutional event, but it doesn't always have to be so. You can pray for your children as you pack their lunches or sing a doxology in the shower. You don't always need a congregation to worship; it's enough that God hears your thanksgiving for this day.

Ever-Deepening Love

As we grow in God's love, we grow in love for others. As His love strengthens us and enables us to do His bidding, so our love for our spouses enables them to be the people God intended them to be.

MARGIE VAWTER

Day 38

For Love

Marrying for love may be a bit risky, but it is so honest that God can't help but smile on it.

JOSH BILLINGS

On the Right Path

You need to listen when your spouse has misgivings about a turn you want to take. You need to consult each other, read the map God has provided, and not allow yourselves to be tempted off the path and into the wilderness.

Day 40

Walk On

There will be days when you, as a couple, will feel others looking at you with disappointment. Perhaps you are having problems in your marriage, or one of your children is going through a rebellious stage, or you have sinned and been found out. You may have tripped, but you can always get up again. Keep your eyes on the Lord, hold your head high, and walk on.

Day 41

A Light

Rejoice not against me, O mine enemy: when I fall, I shall arise; when I sit in darkness, the Lord shall be a light unto me.

Micah 7:8 KJV

Day 42

Invite Him In

God quietly waits through our struggles until we invite Him in. He empathizes with our grief, for He has suffered, too. Day by day, He offers a new vision for our marriage, where He is the center of peace and understanding. He soothes our souls with gentle hands so when we do face disappointment, our hearts will bend toward each other rather than break apart.

SARAH HAWKINS

Thornbushes

Sometimes we all need "thornbushes" to get us right with our mates and Maker. When the stickers prick our skin, we recognize how much we need God—and our spouses—and start reorganizing our lives to reflect that.

Day 44

The Worry Trap

Worrying about money doesn't make you more money. Worrying about love doesn't make you more lovable either. Worry brings you absolutely nothing good. The next time you catch yourself sitting at the kitchen table worrying about something you can't control, go do something useful. It will set your worries free.

Day 45

The "Better" after the "Worse"

More marriages might survive if the partners realized that sometimes the better comes after the worse.

DOUG LARSON

Day 46

Fellowship

A Christian couple needs fellowship with others. They need to see how other Christians are managing their lives. They need the input of older couples whom they can emulate. They need to be part of something bigger than themselves, and they need the love and support of other believers.

God's Design

God didn't make marriage to be painful. He wants to give two people an opportunity to serve Him, enjoy each other, and share happiness and troubles. When we put Him first in our marriages and follow His rules for love, we rejoice in our spouses. Even when we face trouble, God's grace lifts us up and enables us to take delight in our mates.

Day 48

Your Hearts

Could people look at your marriage and identify the two of you as being Christians? Or would they see nothing different about your relationship? Your marriage testifies to the new life that faith in God brings. Your marriage is a physical sign of whatever is in your hearts.

Day 49

Just What We Need

Father, we know You answer our prayers every day, but we don't always see the results or understand Your answers. Whatever Your answer, we have faith that it will be exactly what we need.

Day 50

God Is Waiting

We need wisdom in our relationships, particularly as we strive to grow in godliness and love with our spouses. God is waiting for your prayer, and He desires to guide you in His unsurpassed wisdom. Like little children, we must ask God for help; God will help us find our way.

MANDY NYDEGGER

Overcoming

No matter the circumstances you find yourself in today, God can give your marriage strength and peace. He may not solve every problem overnight, but He'll enable you to overcome each one.

Day 52

Living for Him

As Christians, your peace comes from God. Recognize that daily and you'll see a great change in your emotions for each other. Start praising God together and living for Him, despite your troubles, and your marriage can't help but improve.

Journey with Jesus

A Christian's journey with Jesus—whether walking in His earthly footsteps or following the steps shown us in His Word—is a walk of faith. It's a journey in which seeing isn't believing, but believing is seeing.

Day 54

First Place

Nothing on this earth is truly divine, no matter how much we enjoy it. Nothing, not even a much-loved spouse, can take the place of God in our hearts. Give Jesus first place in your heart and award God a close second. Then you both will win.

Day 55

Investments

Has money taken a place before God, your spouse, and your family? If so, your faith will be weak, your marriage troubled, and your relationships empty. No matter your bank account, you'll be poor. Are you investing in people today or only your financial future?

Day 56

Man and Wife

There is nothing nobler or more admirable than when two people who see eye to eye keep house as man and wife, confounding their enemies and delighting their friends.

HOMER

Realistic Expectations

Scripture tells us that the only One who can meet our every need is God. We can safely hang all our hopes and desires on Him. He never fails. As our Creator, He knows what we need even more than we can imagine. So let's give our [spouses] a break, look at our expectations realistically, and rest in God, waiting for Him to satisfy our deepest needs.

MARGIE VAWTER

Day 58

Direction

A smoothly working team that submits to the needs of each other is wonderful to watch. It has a set goal, and the partners work in rhythm to accomplish it. When they seek to obey God, His will is done, and He is glorified. In what direction is your marriage going?

Marriage Thanks

Thank You, Father, for Your many blessings in our lives. We especially thank You for each other and the love we share.

Day 60

Blessings

Just as we need to thank God for our daily meals, we need to thank Him for our marriages. Enjoying the companionship of another person is a blessing from God, not a weakness.

A Blessing

May your fountain be blessed, and may you rejoice in the wife of your youth.

PROVERBS 5:18 NIV

Day 62

A Third Cord

It's important to have a third cord in your strand of decision making: God. Alone, you can make a devastating wrong choice. But when the Lord of time and space is at the center of your choices, even those that seem less than perfect will turn out fine.

Reaching Out

Every person who knows God is designed to reach out to many. One act by two Christians can even influence a whole world. Are you touching planet Earth today?

Day 64

Gifted

Spiritual gifts aren't meant to start a competition in a marriage, but to benefit others, including your mate. Both of you serve the same Lord, even if your gifts differ. You can use them to reach the world for Christ—or waste time arguing over which set of gifts is "better."

Look Ahead

God wants us to look ahead to the future. The future is where He is. He promises to give us hope in our futures. Let's claim that promise for ourselves, for our spouses, and for our marriages. Let's forget the past—it's long gone already and cannot be changed. Let's move ahead and press toward the new things that the Lord wants to do in our lives.

NICOLE O'DELL

Deal Lovingly

Don't fight over differences. Rather, deal lovingly and intelligently with them, and you'll develop a stronger marriage, fusing your strengths and limiting your weaknesses.

Change and Growth

A good marriage is one which allows for change and growth in the individuals and in the way they express their love.

PEARL S. BUCK

Day 68

Laugh at the Rest

Most of the things that drive us crazy in a marriage were never mentioned in advance. They are truly "hidden" faults, those things a person does without realizing they might bug another. Have patience with each other, change what can be changed, and laugh at the rest.

Harmless Habits

Father, when our hidden faults suddenly appear in our marriage, help us understand that they are mostly harmless, unconscious habits. Help us change what can be changed and accept what cannot be changed.

Day 70

Guard Your Heart

We are to be attentive and careful with what we allow into our hearts and consequently our marriages. We are to shield what we watch on TV, Internet, magazines, and what we allow our minds to dwell on. God tells us to dwell on or think about whatever is true, honorable, just, pure, pleasing, commendable, excellent, and praiseworthy (Philippians 4:8). God will protect and provide peace in our marriages through diligently guarding our hearts.

TINA C. ELACQUA

Just as We Are

God doesn't have bad days or lapses in judgment. We have to assume we are exactly what we were meant to be and go from there. Some things we can improve on; some things we can't. The one thing we can always do is accept God's blessing, just as we are.

Day 72

Imperfections and All

Instead of looking for the imperfections, concentrate on your mate's good qualities, the things that made you fall in love in the first place. Praise those qualities and thank God for bringing you together, imperfections and all.

Up!

The next time you are struggling with temptation and feel yourself sinking into the mud, reach out your hand and ask the Lord to pull you up. He knows how you feel. He's been there.

Day 74

Deliver Me

Willpower has its limits. Don't you believe that the Lord who saved your soul is perfectly capable of helping you turn away from sin? Just ask Him. He knows how to deliver you.

Always Hope

A Christian couple must be able to sustain the same level of hope in their lives, no matter what their current situation. It's not easy when you're playing Russian roulette with the monthly bills or have to send a brilliant child to a trade school instead of the university he or she deserves. But there is always hope.

Prayer Habits

We need to develop effective praying habits for our families. Prayer doesn't have to be locked to a time or a place or a particular posture. We need to kneel in our hearts, whenever we sense the Lord's inner promptings to pray.

SUZANNE WOODS FISHER

Day 77

The Word

Don't read scripture on anyone else's time schedule; rather, make it a natural part of your day together. Whether you open the Book together before you start your day or cuddle up in bed with it before you turn the light out, read it.

Day 78

Measure of Love

This is the true measure of love,
When we believe that we alone can love,
That no one could ever have loved so before us,
And that no one will ever love in the same way after us.

JOHANN WOLFGANG VON GOETHE

Love's Example

Father, neither of us is perfect, and our love is a flawed human love. When we have problems, let us look to You as the example of perfect love we should aim for, even though we know we'll fall short of the mark.

Day 80

Focus

God's Word doesn't just show us how to do something well. Scripture wraps itself around our hearts and fills our lives, changing our way of thinking and our actions. Reading God's Word turns us into new people whose hearts are focused on Him.

God's Truth

Being a witness to God's truth may not always be pleasant. But if you want the people you love to learn the truth and draw close to God, don't hold your tongue. Speak gently and considerately at an opportune time, but do speak.

A "Love" Testimony

No one comes into marriage knowing how to love perfectly. But with time, consideration, and God's tutelage, we learn to make a happy marriage that glorifies our Lord. Comfortingly, we do not go into marriage alone. When we marry in Christ, we are part of a cord of three strands that binds our hearts together (Ecclesiastes 4:12). With the help of our Lord, has our marriage become a testimony to His love?

PAMELA MCQUADE

Love Remains

Many waters cannot quench love;
rivers cannot wash it away.

SONG OF SOLOMON 8:7 NIV

Day 84

Friends

Whether you're giving to a friend or on the receiving end of help, the model you want to follow isn't what the world promotes—it's Jesus' example. When it comes to friends, Jesus is the best One ever.

A Deeper Love

Your husband or wife shares a special, profound love with you, but God loves you even more deeply. No one else can take your place with Him, no matter how many people He saves.

Day 86

His Perfect Timing

Perhaps you've made unwise decisions that are affecting your marriage. Maybe you've fallen into sin and are working your way out of its results. You've turned to God for help, but rescue hasn't been quick in coming. Don't fall prey to bitterness. God isn't finished with your life yet. In His perfect timing, you'll go out full again.

Ready Gifts

Lord, sometimes we get so involved in saving ourselves—in self-improvement, empowerment, and all the current fads—that we forget You are more than willing to help. Help us see our own lack of ability and accept the gifts You give so readily.

Day 88

Goodwill

Kindness is in the life's blood, the elixir of marriage. Kindness makes the difference between passion and caring. Kindness is tenderness. Kindness is love, but perhaps greater than love. . . . Kindness is goodwill. Kindness says, "I want you to be happy." Kindness comes very close to the benevolence of God.

RANDOLPH RAY

Communication

God expects husbands and wives to talk to one another. He wants you to share your fears and insecurities. Be honest and open, freely discussing your desires, needs, and disappointments. Don't clam up when something goes amiss in your relationship. Talk frequently and frankly about every aspect of your couple-hood. After all, if you don't discuss what's on your mind, your spouse will never know.

GALE HYATT

Day 90

Eyes of Faith

God cares when we face troubles that seem to overwhelm us. Our sores may be emotional, not physical, but His 20/20 vision hasn't missed them. Though we may not preview God's plans, we can still trust that they exist. All we need are eyes of faith.

Freedom!

Jesus makes us truly free. When we first believe in Him, we feel swept clean of sin. How wonderful it is to have all the cobwebs dusted from our spirits!

Day 92

An Enormous Advantage

Whatever the years may bring, you do not have to face anything alone. You have a partner and a helper to rejoice with and receive strength from in good times and bad. This gives you an enormous advantage: What one of you cannot do, the other can; what one of you fears, the other does not.

Peace

The couple that shares a belief in Jesus also shares the peace of Jesus—and the mystery of that peace. On the surface such a couple may not seem to have anything but trouble, yet they are happy and content, willing to share the little they do have.

Day 94

Like Eagles

As Christians, when we are weary and worn out, when we have no idea where we will call up the strength to face another day, we still have hope. God promises that when our hope is in Him, we will receive strength to fulfill all the duties He has given us. We will soar above the difficulties like eagles above the storm.

MARGIE VAWTER

Day 95

A Pardon

Accept that your spouse is human, makes mistakes, and falls victim to sin. Understand how much both of you need God's forgiveness and that you may need to mirror His mercy in your married life. Forgiveness isn't a one-way street. Tomorrow you may do something thoughtless and be looking for the same "no strings attached" pardon. You'll be glad it's there.

Day 96

Even More Perfect

The more we love, the more "perfect" Mr. or Mrs. Right becomes. Suddenly the flaws don't seem so large. The things our spouses do well and the spiritual maturity they have attained loom larger than the faults we once "corrected."

Day 97

Lean on God

Influence your mate to stand firm for God. Remind your spouse that God still provides love and support for the hard times. There's nothing the two of you can't get through, if you lean on God.

Transformed

Though you can't ignore marital problems, thinking they'll solve themselves, you can overcome them with God's strength. When His Spirit fills your marriage, you'll avoid some troubles. Instead of despairing, you grow through the trials. As you conform to His likeness, your lives are transformed, and marriage becomes better. And that's a terrific future.

For What You Are

I love you not only for what you are, but for what I am when I am with you. I love you not only for what you have made of yourself, but for what you are making of me. I love you for the part of me that you bring out.

ELIZABETH BARRETT BROWNING

Day 100

Pulling Together

Father, two strong people do not have to pull in opposite directions. When they pull together, with Your help, they can move mountains. Remind us of that the next time we disagree.

Beyond Our Understanding

Good and bad, happy and sad, everything comes from God. We may not like some of the things He gives us, but He has His own reasons beyond our understanding, and everything is part of His plan.

Day 102

A Fine-Tuned Machine

If your relationship has sand in it, wash it out with forgiveness and fill it with kindness and compassion. Don't turn your marriage into a broken-down engine but into a fine-tuned machine for God.

In Agreement

Christian married couples need to find agreement in many positive things: truths we recognize, family goals, and ways in which we can honor God. Are you in agreement today to honor God?

Day 104

Built on the Rock

Just as we look for advice on home-decorating styles, we often follow people with spiritual "styles." It may be a church leader who has a warm personality that draws others to him, a friend who has good values, or someone in the office whom we admire. But unless that person emulates Jesus, by following him or her we may be nicely decorating a house built on sand, instead of making sure we're the contractor for a house built on the Rock.

Spiritual Blessings

Praise be to the God and Father of our Lord Jesus Christ, who has blessed us in the heavenly realms with every spiritual blessing in Christ.

EPHESIANS 1:3 NIV

Day 106

Like Seashells

The secret to contentment comes from understanding that where we are now is exactly where God wants us to be. He has a purpose for our lives and He offers a peace that is separate from our circumstances. When we open our hearts to this, then love comes rushing in the way the tide fills even the tiniest holes in the sand and blessings are scattered around like seashells.

SARAH HAWKINS

Love Alone

Love alone is capable of uniting living beings in such a way as to complete and fulfill them, for it alone takes them and joins them by what is deepest in themselves.

PIERRE TEILHARD DE CHARDIN

Day 108

Sacrifice

Sacrifice is required in marriage. . . . You may not say you are sacrificing for love. But that's the reason you do it: because of love. Your marriage is more important to you than a night out or a weekend game. You are living a life of love.

Bless This Marriage

Dear Jesus, we want Your blessing on our marriage. Show us how to abide in You individually and as a couple.

MARILEE PARRISH

Day 110

Trust

God provides all the solutions for our lives, whether it's rain to bring relief to a parched land or arid, clear days that dry out a wet home. He heals unhappy relationships and can cure illnesses doctors can't even identify. All we have to do is ask and trust in Him.

Creative Ways

God's Word wasn't meant to be shut up in your hearts. If it doesn't affect your actions, it isn't serving its best purpose. There are many creative ways you can reach out together with God's truth. Plan to do that today.

Day 112

Richest Sacrifice

God does not change; God always deserves praise. Today, give Him your richest sacrifice as you glorify Him, despite life's challenges.

TLC

Drooping leaves on a houseplant indicate that it needs some attention, and when the quality of your marriage begins to droop, it's time to focus on some TLC. Discuss your relationship over a candlelight dinner. Air your grievances. Reaffirm your commitment to one another. Catching problems and nipping them in the bud before they can bloom into serious issues will go a long way to keeping your marriage lush and beautiful.

GALE HYATT

DAY 114

Faith's Benefits

You may not be a perfect mate, but if you walk closely with God, as you become more like Him, you'll be more caring and forgiving. Both you and your spouse will see faith's benefits.

By Love

Love is a flame that burns in heaven, and whose soft reflections radiate to us. Two worlds are opened, two lives given to it. It is by love that we double our being: It is by love that we approach God.

AIMEE MARTIN

Day 116

Secrets

Random acts of kindness are never planned and seldom rewarded by those around us at the time. They are secrets between two people and God. But God remembers them, and they will be rewarded.

Give of Yourselves

Father, we may or may not have the means to give generously to charity, but we all have the ability to give of ourselves. When we do, help us not to seek or expect the praise of others. You see. That's enough.

Day 118

When All Else Fails

Only God is eternal and never changing, the One who holds us up and never betrays our trust. Only God gives us hope in our darkest moments when all else has failed.

Clear the Air

If you don't already, challenge yourself to pray nightly with your companion. That way, if any ill feelings have accumulated throughout the day, you'll have a chance to air them before you turn out the lights.

GALE HYATT

Day 120

In Spite of Ourselves

At the end of a bad day, our spouses bear the brunt of our disappointments and defeats. Why do they put up with us? Because they understand, they know our true hearts, and they love us in spite of ourselves.

God's Love

When you are feeling far away from God, remember that He knows and loves you even more than your spouse does. He anticipates your wants and needs, just as your spouse does, and always wants to please you.

Day 122

Joyful Forgiveness

Father, Your forgiveness and the joy it brings us are examples of the way we should treat our partners when we disagree or have our feelings hurt. Remind us of that the next time we feel wounded by the other.

Reflection

Like the way light pours through a diamond, God's light reflects best through the love we offer to others, especially to our spouses. We are not to be hidden away for safekeeping, for only in use do the jewels of compassion, kindness, gentleness, and patience sparkle brightly against a dark and colorless world.

SARAH HAWKINS

Day 124

Listen

Listen to your spouse with as much attention and affection as you listened while you were dating, and you may find your love is deeper than you ever imagined.

Closer Together

Lord, remind us that true love is shown in the daily business of living. It may not be romantic, but it brings us together and shows us exactly what You mean love to be: service to others.

Day 126

Fruit of the Spirit

When we focus on Jesus, changes happen in our lives. While we're not even looking—because we have our eyes on Him—we start experiencing an unexpected fruit of the Spirit. We are obeying Him in one place, and He gives us an unanticipated gift.

Day 127

Author and Perfecter of Faith

Therefore, since we have so great a cloud of witnesses surrounding us, let us also lay aside every encumbrance. . .fixing our eyes on Jesus, the author and perfecter of faith.

HEBREWS 12:1–2 NASB

Day 128

Sweetness

Love is something like the clouds that were in the sky before the sun came out. . . . You cannot touch the clouds, you know; but you feel the rain and know how glad the flowers and the thirsty earth are to have it after a hot day. You cannot touch love either, but you feel the sweetness that it pours into everything.

ANNE SULLIVAN

Rejoice Together

Have you had time to be alone with your spouse? If not, the strains of marital life may begin to get the best of you. Take time for a date night or afternoon. Enjoy a nice romantic dinner, a quick takeout in the park, or share the beauties of nature on an afternoon walk. Whatever you do, rejoice together in the relationship God gave you.

PAMELA MCQUADE

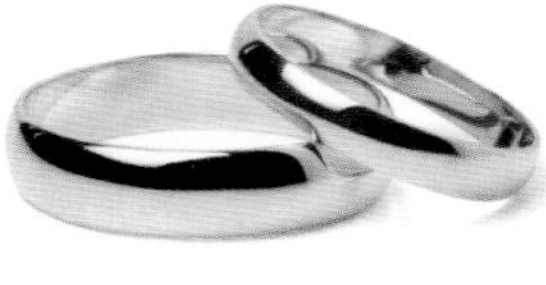

Day 130

Tuned In

If we praise God—in our homes, at church, or in the marketplace—we may run into people who don't like it. But we'll also bless hurting people. Hearing about Jesus can lift the saddest heart, when it's tuned in to His praise.

Romance

Treat your spouse with constant love, and you'll develop a great friendship—and a terrific romance.

Day 132

With Love

The next time you and your spouse disagree, remember the Lord's reaction to disappointment. Stun your spouse with love.

Primary Place

God wants very much to be involved in our lives. He wants to be included in every aspect of our marriages, families, careers, and so forth. Great God that He is, He still cares for each of us individually. How about it? Will *you* let Him have the primary place in your home?

RACHEL QUILLIN

Shine

Think for a moment about a lighthouse. Shining a powerful beam across the waters, this beacon of light does a pretty good job, even if its windows are salt-encrusted and it does nothing more than just stand there on the rocks. Sometimes that's all we need to do: stand faithfully on the Rock and shine the best we can.

Through Tough Times

No one wants to go through hard times. We'd rather learn to abound and be full, but if God is with us, we can do anything. Perhaps the most important thing we can learn from hard times is that God stays with us through them all and brings us out of them in His time.

Day 136

Joyful Homes

Because of life's disappointments, we can lose our pleasure in God's company. . . . We must work to regain that closeness so that we will be at peace and not causing contention. When we find joy in God, we are more apt to find joy in our spouse. With time and prayer we begin to look forward to time with God and our spouse. Imagine how joyful our homes will be then.

NANCY FARRIER

Constant, Faithful Love

Father, Your constant and faithful love will bring us through any trial we may have to face. When times are good again, we will not forget the strength You gave us in our darkest moments.

Day 138

Change Yourself First

If you want to change your spouse, change yourself first. If you win the argument by getting what you want, but do damage to your relationship by hurting trust and respect, have you really won? As always, prayer is the best way to refocus your heart and mind onto the ways of God.

NICOLE O'DELL

As Simple and Difficult

Love one another and you will be happy.
It's as simple and difficult as that.

MICHAEL LEUNIG

Day 140

The True Nature of Love

Love is always changing, never static. It grows and matures as we do. Love is giving, not taking; forgiving, not abandoning. As people change, so does the nature of their love.

God's Faithfulness

Today, with your spouse, share ways that you have seen God's faithfulness. Has He given you a new freedom in life, brought you through financial trials, or worked in a surprising way?

Day 142

Strength to Forgive

Lord, when we fight unfairly with each other and intentionally hurt each other, give us the strength we need to forgive, no matter how hard that is to do.

Dreams

It's hard to wait for your dreams to be realized, but when you talk to God about them, He'll bring them about in a way you never imagined, and you'll be surprised when you find you and your spouse going in the same direction—down the same path—sharing the dream that God has for your lives—together!

SHANNA GREGOR

Day 144

At Peace

Father, even when we confess our sins to You and receive Your forgiveness, we may not be able to confess them to each other. Don't let the past ruin our present. Help us accept Your forgiveness and be at peace with our past.

Flame of Love

Prosper today by listening carefully to God's Word and acting it out in your lives. Then the flame of His love will burn in your hearts and not destroy you.

Love Never Fails

Love is patient, love is kind. It does not envy, it does not boast, it is not proud. It is not rude, it is not self-seeking, it is not easily angered, it keeps no record of wrongs. Love does not delight in evil but rejoices with the truth. It always protects, always trusts, always hopes, always perseveres. Love never fails.

1 CORINTHIANS 13:4–8 NIV

What Is Love?

Love.
What is love?
No one can define it.
It's something so great, only God could design it.
Yes, love is beyond what man can define.
For love is immortal. And God's gift is divine.

HELEN STEINER RICE

Day 148

Honeymoon Love

Seek forgiveness and healing together, instead of indulging in anger and calamities, and your relationship can deepen. You can't live on honeymoon love forever, but you can keep calamities at bay.

Transformed

God can transform our marriages when we have God's attitude of the heart of forgiveness. God knows we are not able to forgive the hurt and pain in our marriage without His supernatural power. Jesus said, ". . .whatever you ask for in prayer, believe that you have received it, and it will be yours" (Mark 11:24). When we ask Him, God promises to give us the ability through the power of the Holy Spirit to have this attitude of the heart—forgiveness.

TINA C. ELACQUA

Day 150

Slow to Anger

We can trust in the God who is slow to anger because we have experienced His mercy. When we err or even sin intentionally, He is also slow to retaliate so that we can have time to come to Him in repentance. Aren't we all glad swift justice is not always His?

The Right Track

If joy and laughter fill your home, you're on the right track. If you've always taken life completely seriously, it's time to let down your guard and loosen up a bit. Decide to do some genuine laughing. You'll be glad you did.

RACHEL QUILLIN

Gift of God

Remember that a marriage concerns three people, not two, and the Lord gave you your spouse and knows exactly how you feel. He wants your marriage to thrive. Give Him time to help you. Don't toss away a gift of God.

The Right Perspective

The Lord knows we all have wishes and dreams, but He wants us to have the right perspective on them and not let them control our lives or make us act irrationally. Wish for anything you want; covet nothing.

Day 154

Deepest Love Needs

No human being can love us the way God intends for us to be loved. When we look to our spouse to provide that love, we will be disappointed time and time again. Only God can fill the void in our heart. When we learn to allow God's love to seep into our deepest places and fill our deepest needs, our human relationships become transformed. . .because we are allowing God to meet our deepest love needs.

JOANNA BLOSS

The Beautiful

The best and most beautiful things in this world cannot be seen or touched but must be felt with the heart.

HELEN KELLER

Lover of My Soul

Father, You are the Lover of my soul. You alone can meet all my needs—help me to accept Your love so that I can love others with purity and grace. Amen.

JOANNA BLOSS

Rewards

The next time you give of your resources, try doing so in secret and see how much more rewarding your gift will feel to you.

Prayer First

The next time you find yourself bickering with your spouse, remember that God is not the author of confusion and that He brings peace and harmony to all situations. Join with your spouse in prayer, surrendering your individual wills, asking for God's guidance. It will be impossible to resume the bickering after refocusing and turning it over to the Lord.

NICOLE O'DELL

God's Offer

If you are facing hard times, accept God's offer to be your Father. Bring your problems to Him, listen for His advice, and know you are still loved.

Reconnect

Why not set aside a day to reconnect with God as a couple? Pray together and talk about all of the little things that made you fall in love in the first place. Ask forgiveness from the Lord for getting out of touch with Him and ask Him to fill you up and be the center of your life and marriage.

MARILEE PARRISH

Fan That Flame

Relationships require a lot of maintenance. Your marriage won't survive on the back burner. No matter how hectic life may be, take time for your spouse. Don't allow outside commitments to distract you from the person who matters most. Keep the flame of your marriage fanned and you'll never have to worry about your love growing cold.

GALE HYATT

Day 162

Just What We Need

Life provides us with plenty to deal with in one day, so why look ahead to tomorrow's problems? God knows exactly what we need and will provide it when we need it. That should leave us all with a little extra time to "seek. . .first the kingdom of God, and his righteousness" (Matthew 6:33 KJV).

Tomorrow

Take therefore no thought for the morrow: for the morrow shall take thought for the things of itself. Sufficient unto the day is the evil thereof.

MATTHEW 6:34 KJV

Day 164

Our Burden Bearer

With every anxiety God calls us to throw everything on Him, to let go of the burden of worry, large or small. He wants to be our burden bearer because He is able, because He cares for us affectionately and watchfully. He knows the burden of anxiety we carry. Roll it off onto His mighty shoulders today.

MARGIE VAWTER

God's Capable Hands

Change is a funny thing. It is always there breathing underneath the surface of our lives. Our job is simply to love our [spouses] and put the work of change in God's capable hands. After all, He loves more and sees more than we do.

SARAH HAWKINS

Day 166

Glimpse of Eternity

The story of love is not important—what is important is that one is capable of love. It is perhaps the only glimpse we are permitted of eternity.

HELEN HAYES

Faith in God's Provision

Father, we trust You for the basics of life but continue to worry about them, as if our worrying could do us any good. Strengthen our faith in Your provision so we can concentrate on the work You have in mind for us to accomplish.

True Peace

We can find true peace when we spend time with God. That may be in a special service, but we also need time together with Him in prayer and His Word. If we're attempting to do God's will without tapping directly into Him, we're out of His will, however busy we are. We need to spend time today resting in Him alone.

Fulfilled

When we choose to make our focus pleasing God, it doesn't matter what people say about us if we fail to please others. Only in pleasing God, being obedient to His commands and guidelines for life, especially in our marriage relationships, do we truly feel fulfilled and content.

MARGIE VAWTER

The World

The world will try to pull our eyes away from Jesus. Staying faithful to reading and meditating on God's Word will keep our eyes focused where they should be, on the Author and Perfecter of our faith.

LAURA FREUDIG

A Masterpiece

Do we bang away and clash against each other hoping one side will change, or do we search for God's perspective and make the necessary shift so that His design is revealed? In time, we will see that our marriage was designed to be His masterpiece here on earth.

SARAH HAWKINS

Day 172

Sharing Love

Two who share both human love and God's love have the best of this world and the next. Draw close to Him today.

Rest

Thank You, Lord, for being our rest. When life gets too hectic, remind us that we need to stop what we're doing and rest in You.

Day 174

Risking Everything

Love is everything it's cracked up to be. . . . It really is worth fighting for, being brave for, risking everything for.

ERICA JONG

Satisfyingly Loved

You are loved deeply and satisfyingly by God.
He has never forgotten you, and He never will.

Day 176

Unexpected Blessing

Are you and your spouse feeling very "unblessed" today? Perhaps that unexpected blessing from God is just around the corner. When it comes, His blessing may impact more than you and your family alone. People will call you blessed if you remain faithful to Him in your trials.

Your Words

It's impossible to speak the right words if we're not thinking the right thoughts. The things we think about every day will eventually come out in our conversations. Those thoughts can emerge in words that can hurt others or encourage them, words that lift them up or tear them down. Since this process begins in our minds, it is essential for us to filter our thoughts through God's Word so that the words *we* speak will glorify Him.

JOANNA BLOSS

Day 178

Every Provision

Trust God to provide; rest in His love. And thank Him for every provision. God loves to receive our worship for what we often take for granted.

MARGIE VAWTER

Recipe for Marriage

A godly marriage cannot do without any of the things that God has ordained for it. All of the ingredients that God has included in His recipe are vital for our marriages. Take a moment to consider which area in your marriage needs some remeasuring. The results will be well worth the effort!

NICOLE O'DELL

Day 180

Each Step of the Way

Spend some time in prayer. Praise God for the good things He has done for you and the opportunities you have had for growth. Thank Him for being with you each step of the way.

In Charge

When God is in charge, He brings amazing things to pass. People who don't even believe in Him may cause His will to happen for Christians. Seemingly impossible situations suddenly change. A knotty problem disappears. When our lives are out of control, it's time to put them in the control of the One who rules all.

Day 182

In Motion

Ultimately, God should be in control of each area of your marriage and life together. If you've been in control and have not let Him rule in your lives, identify where you need to change and how you can do it. Set some plans in motion today.

Adaptation

When "life" seems to interrupt your plans, do you complain or adapt? Can you see it as part of God's plan and not just an irritant? God might use that interruption to create a great moment in your life.

Day 184

Darkness to Light

I will bring the blind by a way that they knew not; I will lead them in paths that they have not known: I will make darkness light before them, and crooked things straight. These things will I do unto them, and not forsake them.

ISAIAH 42:16 KJV

Never Alone

God promises to do the impossible for His blind, stressed people: He will give light to those who don't even know what it is. He will straighten our paths in ways we could never envision. Just as a faithful friend guides a blind person through a dangerous intersection in a strange city, God will help us deal with the unknown. He never leaves us alone.

RACHAEL PHILLIPS

Day 186

Amazing Grace

Even though we all go through difficult times in marriage, there isn't a relationship that can't be restored by our loving Father and turned into a testimony of His amazing grace! Sometimes the difficult relationships turn into an even greater legacy because of how God has been glorified through our weaknesses. Pray with your spouse today. Share your desire to leave a legacy for your loved ones, and take your desires to the Lord together in prayer.

MARILEE PARRISH

How He Loves Us

God wants us to love each other in spite of our faults. Because that's how He loves us. He is constantly forgiving us and enduring our shortcomings.

DONNA MALTESE

Day 188

Real Function

Love is something eternal—the aspect may change, but not the essence. There is the same difference in a person before and after he is in love as there is in an unlighted lamp and one that is burning. The lamp was there and it was a good lamp, but now it is shedding light, too, and that is its real function.

VINCENT VAN GOGH

Promises Kept

If you can trust that God gave His Son, you can trust Him when He moves you to change jobs, take a spiritual risk, or give unselfishly. He hasn't broken a promise yet, and He won't start with you.

Lifelong Romance

Scripture teaches us that married people who follow God's Word have the real freedom—they've been freed by the Spirit to develop a single deep relationship. Each member of a Christian couple focuses on loving the other deeply and uniquely. As both work to build a godly relationship, these committed married folks develop real, lifelong romance.

PAMELA MCQUADE

Obedience

What challenges to obedience do each of you face? Discuss those things that make it hard for you and how you can overcome them. Then spend time together in prayer, seeking the solutions God has to offer.

Day 192

A Good Marriage

There is no more lovely, friendly, and charming relationship, communion, or company than a good marriage.

MARTIN LUTHER

Day 193

Sacrificial Love

Jesus loved us when we were sinners. Before we knew Him and had been changed, He loved us enough to die for us. What a beautiful example of sacrificial love in action. As followers of Christ, we, too, can learn to have a sacrificial love in our marriages. When our feelings for our spouse begin to fade, we can remember the way Jesus gave His all for us, and follow in His footsteps.

NANCY FARRIER

Day 194

Growing Together

Lord, we realize that we are stronger and smarter when we work together on a problem. Please remind us of this anytime we are tempted to "take over" or impose our own ways on each other. Help us use our own particular talents to grow as a team.

Name ______________________

Address ______________________

____

______________ Tel (   ) ______________

e-mail ______________________

- [ ] Please send free catalogue and details of mail order
- [ ] Please send details on Representatives & Distributors
- [ ] Please e-mail info regularly about new products

Book Title ______________________

Bought at ______________________

Comments ______________________

____

____

____

AFFIX POSTAGE

Mail to:
Living Books Inc.

Box 142
Borden, SK
S0K 0N0

Strong Foundation

If you can get over little problems, you will have the foundation of a strong marriage. Still, patience and perseverance are required: You need to come to acceptable compromises without becoming weary and, at the same time, keep working on the little issues that drive you crazy.

Day 196

How to Love

When we demand something from our spouse that he or she cannot deliver immediately, our first reaction is to turn away, to not be patient. When we learn to be patient, we will learn how to love—even when we do not receive what we think we want.

His Marvelous Light

Perhaps you are facing a dark situation right now. Maybe you've suffered loss, a moral failure, or missed a chance to defend your faith. If so, you're not alone—you have a lot of company. When it seems that you're surrounded by darkness, remember that light is both your foundation and your future. Release the situation to God's marvelous light and know that He is able to transform it into something more than you could ever dream.

JOANNA BLOSS

Your Own Path

It is important to remember that the place you are creating with your spouse is *your own*. Glean the good from your parents' marriages, but make sure you leave plenty of room to blaze your own path.

GALE HYATT

Courage to Persevere

Be prepared to pray earnestly as you work to maintain a marriage that glorifies God. And know that it is a fight to the finish, one that doesn't end this side of heaven. It takes courage to persevere in the face of spiritual opposition.

MARGIE VAWTER

Day 200

Buggy

Those we love can drive us buggy, and two people can disagree on what is important. When that happens to you, do you have the grace to give in with a smile and bring peace to the family?

Shared Secret

Father, sometimes the simplest gifts are too complex to comprehend. Whenever possible, help us share the secret of our contentment with those who do not understand Your peace and blessings.

Day 202

"I Will Do It"

"And I will do whatever you ask in my name, so that the Son may bring glory to the Father. You may ask me for anything in my name, and I will do it."

JOHN 14:13–14 NIV

Some Days. . .

Some days it may seem that the world—or at least one person—is highly disappointed by how we turned out. We can't do anything right. And by the time the day is over, we're ready to call it quits and go to sleep. You are not alone. You have your spouse to lean on in times of trouble, as well as the heavenly Father, who knew you before you were even born.

Tempered by Hope

A Christian family will suffer as much grief as any other family. Loss will hurt them just as deeply. The difference is, a Christian's grief is always tempered by hope.

Leaving a Mark

No love. . .can cross the path of our destiny without leaving some mark on it forever.

FRANÇOIS MAURIAC

Day 206

Into the Presence of God

Do whatever you can to make time to pray together as a couple. Pencil it into your daily schedule, record it in your Blackberry, send yourself an e-mail. . .whatever you need to do. Prayer ushers us into the presence of God. Prayer allows us to hear and echo the needs of our spouse. Prayer changes things.

MARILEE PARRISH

Energy

Where do you put your energy? Are you focused on the right things for a healthy marriage? Take a good look at the distractions that have come between you and a successful relationship with your spouse. Set aside time to really focus on your relationship.

SHANNA GREGOR

Day 208

Self-Control

Father, I know very well how to hurt my partner, to find that one weak spot that is the most tender and vulnerable. When I am feeling hurt and unloved, give me the self-control not to say the words that will hurt the most.

Other Viewpoints

Don't fall into the "I'm in charge here" trap. You need each other's viewpoints to handle successfully the troubles that will come your way.

Day 210

Mutual Respect

Mutual respect is the foundation of a good marriage. Two different people may have legitimate opposing views on any subject, from how to handle money to which football team to support. Of importance is not the issue but how you treat each other.

Smoother Relationships

Couples who pray fervently for each other rediscover improved marital communication. Through prayer, suddenly both understand each other more clearly. As the Spirit works in their lives, they feel His oil on the rough parts of their relationship. So don't forget to pray!

PAMELA MCQUADE

God's Protection

We don't always have fences around our houses, and even if we did, they couldn't protect our families from everything. But what we do have is a promise from God that He stands eternal sentry over those who love Him.

LAURA FREUDIG

Day 213

The Best Thing

Love is not getting, but giving. . . . It is goodness and honor and peace and pure living—yes, love is that, and it is the best thing in the world and the thing that lives the longest.

HENRY VAN DYKE

Experience

Experience is the best teacher in any case and especially in marriage. Reading every book ever written by experts on relationships can't teach you what simple failure can. Mistakes are embarrassing, often painful, and can send you spiraling into depression. But the wealth of knowledge gained from them will make you a better spouse. Don't despair over your goofs and gaffes. Learn from them and keep that knowledge handy. You never know when you'll need it next.

GALE HYATT

Depth

Thank You, Father, for showing us the joy of married love. Help us to take time today to express the depth of emotion that we share.

Before Perfection

Like God, who loved us even when we had no thought of Him, we must love our spouses *before* they become perfect. We need to encourage them to seek God's will and overcome flaws, but we need to love them during the process.

Wedded Bliss!

God designed marriage to be a delightful experience shared by a man and woman. The power of wedded bliss to intoxicate goes far beyond wine yet lacks wine's harmful properties. Today is a good time to remember how much your spouse means to you and to appreciate the love God has given you.

Day 218

Extravagantly

God not only gives to us; He gives extravagantly. He offered up His Son, the dearest gift He had to give. Anything else seems small in comparison. And God keeps on giving good gifts—and only good gifts—all the time.

Brought to Light

God wants to be able to shine through us and through our marriages. To do our part, we must allow Him to show us areas where we harbor bad attitudes or hurts. When those are brought to light and dealt with, then we can truly radiate God's love.

NANCY FARRIER

Day 220

God's Plan and Purpose

Lord, thank You for my marriage. Let my influence always steer us toward Your plan and purpose. Amen.

One Purpose

Don't be afraid to ask your spouse the hard questions like: Do you feel like I am meeting your needs? Do you feel loved and respected by me? What are your personal goals for life and for our marriage? These conversations may be difficult but they will most definitely help you get your marriage back to "one purpose."

MARILEE PARRISH

Day 222

Useful Vessels

God, the Master Potter, knows exactly what to do to expose the weaknesses and strengths of each vessel. He never leaves us to work out our problems alone, nor does He repair our cracks with imperfect glue. We may suffer, but God is ready to do what is necessary to make us useful vessels once again.

MARGIE VAWTER

Encouragement and Love

Is your spouse facing a trial? Don't dump a negative message on your mate. Instead, lift him or her up with encouragement and love.

The Best Medicine

Keeping your mind on the most positive things you can contemplate is like taking a wonder drug—in other words, good medicine—that puts zip back into your step. The best medicine or dried-up bones can testify to your faith. Which will it be?

A Merry Heart

A merry heart does good, like medicine, but a broken spirit dries the bones.

PROVERBS 17:22 NKJV

Love Changes Hearts

Father, unloving people can take the shine out of our days. Help us to love them as much as they let us, and keep us praying until love changes hearts.

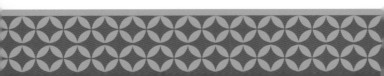

God Bless the One

God bless the [one] who sees my needs
and reaches out a hand,
Who lifts me up, who prays for me,
and helps me understand.

AMANDA BRADLEY

Leftovers

Thank God for giving you the grace to give to those in need around you, and watch Him rain down blessings. Even the *leftovers* will be more abundant than we can imagine.

LAURA FREUDIG

DAY 229

Jumping to Conclusions

We've all been guilty of jumping to conclusions before we have all the information. We make judgments and decisions based on what we *think* might have happened, or what we have seen happen in the past. Assumptions like these can get us into trouble because often there is more to the story. Ask questions, be patient. . .it may keep you from having to apologize later.

JOANNA BLOSS

Day 230

Big Enough

Whether you need money to pay the bills or answers for how to deal with balky teenagers, you've probably prayed a "Help, quick!" prayer to God. Everyone has those moments when nothing on earth, not even our much-loved spouses, seems to answer the need. Only God is big enough for this trouble.

Time Management

Take this day and use it for God. Bless your spouse and family. Make wise choices. Only then will you have properly numbered the day.

Day 232

Best Interests

Lord, our evaluation of our friends is not always accurate. Thank You for giving us someone who always has our best interests at heart, and make us willing to consider the advice our spouse offers.

Changing Your Outlook

Sometimes in life trials hit us from every side. We find ourselves tense and disoriented, wanting to take control even when we know God is there watching out for us. The race we are running becomes more than we can bear as we see obstacles we hadn't counted on in front of us. This is when we must take a deep breath and focus on Jesus. By changing our outlook from the stumbling blocks to Jesus, we will begin to relax and allow Him to handle the adversities.

NANCY FARRIER

Bright Colors

Can our spouses testify to the light shining through our lives? Do the robes of Jesus shine whitely, or has sin muddied the picture, blocking His light from our witness? As Jesus influences our marriages, our paths shine, first in the power of dawn sunshine, then ever increasing, till a more-than-noonday brightness enlivens all the colors of our picture window.

PAMELA MCQUADE

The Simple Way

Each of us needs a relationship with at least one other person who also seeks and trusts the simple way, the Simple Presence [of God].

TILDEN H. EDWARDS

Day 236

Because You Believe

Perhaps some of your prayers have been answered so fast it frightened you. Others you can see becoming answered one step at a time. Still others have not yet been answered or were answered in ways you cannot see or understand. But one way or another, your prayers are being heard and answered, because you believe.

DAY 237

A New Day

It's hard to glorify God while concentrating on shaving or trying to get everyone up and out on time. No one has time for more than the bare essentials at dawn, but the beginning of a new day is a precious gift that should be welcomed and for which we should give thanks.

Let Your Life Shine

As you point others to God, to His light—His goodness, mercy, and love—your light shines, repelling darkness and bringing comfort to everyone God brings across your path. How encouraging to know that your life can brighten the whole room. You have the power to open the door of someone's heart for the Holy Spirit to speak to them about their own salvation. Don't miss a moment to let your life shine!

SHANNA GREGOR

More Clearly

Through Jesus we understand ourselves and each other more clearly. Jesus cleans out the dirty spaces in our hearts and gives us true joy. He can make marriage wonderful, but no marriage—even one provided and blessed by Him—can fill the places He fills in our hearts.

Covered Weakness

Sometimes weakness can be devastating to a marriage. But Jesus loves you regardless of your weakness, and He is there to provide His strength at all times. Ask Him for the strength to do the right thing. His grace is enough to cover your weakness, and He is glorified in the process!

MARILEE PARRISH

Consideration

Teamwork isn't a matter of one partner driving the other but of two pulling in the same direction God has set for them. As they move in the same direction, in service to Him, they take each other into consideration. And that marriage grows.

Day 242

Nothing to Fear

Father, help us build trust in each other as the years go by, until we are totally comfortable with each other and know we have nothing to fear from the one we love.

Your Vine

Some discouraging periods are mercifully short, but others can go on for a long time. How do you cope with them? All you can do is cling to the Lord, your vine, and know that somehow, someday, you will be fruitful and accomplish His purpose for your life. Until then, it's your job to hang in there with all your might and live in faith and hope.

Day 244

Your Beloved

Don't let the busyness of this world keep you from focusing in on the beloved in your life. Leave e-mail behind, turn the cell phones off, and get away for a day, a weekend, or a week—somewhere far from the responsibilities of home, work, and family.

DONNA MALTESE

Look to God

Our true source of hope and joy comes in knowing the Lord. He is the One who won't leave us or forsake us. God is always there. He understands our hurts from the inside out. Only God can truly empathize with our loneliness or disillusionment with life. God sees our heart and knows our intent. This is something our spouse can never fully do. When we learn to look to God for our joy, then we will be happy in our marriage, too.

NANCY FARRIER

Day 246

Godly Wisdom

Not all advice is good advice. But the Bible encourages us to seek godly wisdom. If there's a wrinkle in your relationship that you can't seem to smooth out, don't be afraid or ashamed to ask for help. A few healthy tips from the right people can make a world of difference in your marriage.

GALE HYATT

Safety

In the multitude of counselors there is safety.

PROVERBS 11:14 NKJV

Day 248

Life Decisions

The next time you have to make a life decision, take a minute to think about how that decision will affect your future. Riches can't give you eternal life, but Jesus can and will.

From Love

Miracles occur naturally as expressions of love. The real miracle is the love that inspires them. In this sense everything that comes from love is a miracle.

MARIANNE WILLIAMSON

Day 250

Giving

Money, slick advertisements, and careful plans aren't what it takes to spread the gospel of Jesus Christ. Belief in God is the critical element. Though faithful giving to groups with ambitious goals is not wrong, we need to recognize that money doesn't run the organization—God does. Where He blesses obedience, provision appears for those who go and those who organize.

Follow Through

If you really love God, don't only read His Word—follow through on it, too. Then the world will know you're committed, and you won't deceive anyone—least of all yourself.

Day 252

For the Good of Marriage

Lord, help us to be kind and gentle when we point out each other's weaknesses, but help us to say the words that need to be spoken for the good of our marriage.

Always Ready

Jesus never wasted a moment or passed up an opportunity to do what was right. He took breaks, He went to quiet places to pray, and He fed his soul with rest, but He was always ready to do His Father's work. If we feed our souls with the Word, go to our quiet places to pray, and get rest as we let the Holy Spirit minister to us, we will be prepared to tackle our Father's work in our homes and in the world.

NICOLE O'DELL

Day 254

For His Great Purpose

When we believe that God has brought us together for His great purpose, then we know our marriage is stronger than the arguments that threaten to pull us apart. God uses friction to erode away our rough edges, the way water meets land and carves new landscapes. His presence is rain in a drought—full of a freshness that even charred and blackened hearts can absorb. And out of the ashes new dreams rise up in a downpour of God's love.

SARAH HAWKINS

Hope for Children

What is the greatest hope you have for your children? Isn't it that no matter what they become or accomplish, they will be happy? How can you teach them that? Your children may be rich or poor, famous or humble, but only God's peace will bring them true happiness.

Day 256

Constant, Abiding Love

Lord, in a disappointing, human world, You are our strength, the One we turn to when we are alone and afraid. Thank You for Your constant, abiding love that brightens our lives.

Rare Indeed

Perfect love is rare indeed—for to be a lover will require that you continually have the subtlety of the very wise, the flexibility of the child, the sensitivity of the artist, the understanding of the philosopher, the acceptance of the saint, the tolerance of the scholar, and the fortitude of the certain.

LEO BUSCAGLIA

Day 258

Always Right There

Even the best Christians have days when God seems to be concentrating on the other side of the world. . .but God is always right there, just behind our shoulders, covering our backs and providing everything He promised to provide. He is always faithful, even when our emotions cause us to doubt that faithfulness.

Taste His Peace

Life is not neat. It's full of disorder, loose ends, and unresolved conflicts that keep us from feeling at peace. There's no point at which we can clap our hands and say, "There! . . . That part of our life is over!" The next time you are overwhelmed by life's disorder, place it all in God's hand and taste His peace.

Overflowing Love

When we allow God's Spirit to work freely in our lives, we'll rarely have a love problem. Overflowing love will surround us, helping us in every need. All we need do is reach for Him.

PAMELA MCQUADE

The Gift

The gift of marriage is meant for us to learn many of life's lessons. Lessons of love, joy, loss, pain, trust, forgiveness, peace, contentment. . .these lessons are gifts from the Father meant for us to experience and learn from during marriage.

MARILEE PARRISH

Details

No marriage is perfect—some are better than others, but all marriages take work to keep them healthy and functioning within the guidelines of scripture. Knowing God is aware of the details of our marriages can bring comfort and strength to keep working. It's a blessing to know that God preordained our positions, trusting us to work with our spouses to maintain a marriage that honors Him.

MARGIE VAWTER

Seek His Face

Hear my voice when I call, O Lord; be merciful to me and answer me. My heart says of you, "Seek his face!" Your face, Lord, I will seek.

Psalm 27:7–8 NIV

Best Friends

When the kids are grown and gone, leaving the two of you to rattle around the house alone, you may make the astounding discovery that your best friend is your spouse. Such a discovery usually comes as a surprise. The passion of youth may have faded, and you've certainly had your share of arguments and disagreements, but the one you trust and love the most is still the same. What a joy to grow old with your best friend!

Real-Life Romance

Romance is wonderful, but reality is even more so. The next time you feel that love has grown cold in your marriage, remember all the daily sacrifices your spouse has made for the sake of the family. Hanging in there for all those years is (extremely) romantic!

Day 266

Love's Fabric

Love is a fabric which never fades, no matter how often it is washed in the water of adversity and grief.

ANONYMOUS

Home and Family

Dear heavenly Father, thank You for my home and family. Help me to always cherish it and to care for it as You would have me to. Amen.

GALE HYATT

Strengthened Bond

God knows the trials we face in our marriages. He understands the difficulties and is right there with us. What we must remember is that we have His promise, as prisoners of hope, that He will restore double to us when we come through each trial. As we rely on Him to get us through, we can expect our bond to strengthen to the point where we won't be torn apart.

NANCY FARRIER

Unburdened Hearts

Got trouble? Get talking. Pour out your heart before the Lord. He is ready and waiting to listen. Give Him the desires of your heart. Leave your troubles at His feet. And then, knowing all is in His hands, worship Him, letting your newly unburdened heart rejoice!

DONNA MALTESE

Day 270

Choosing Together

God has the whole world in His hands, but daily choices belong to you. Choose to live in His will, making decisions with your spouse based on His direction that comes from a personal relationship—time spent with Him in prayer and in His Word. Jesus knew the path set before Him, and you can, too. Choose today.

SHANNA GREGOR

His Majesty

God isn't just a pretty personality. He also has unlimited splendor, majesty, and strength. The more you look at Him, the more there is to see. Have you looked at Him today and seen His strength? Have you seen His splendor and worshipped His majesty? Come close to Him today.

Day 272

Reality Check

Telling the truth in marriage can be particularly hard. After all, you can't stage a "truth attack" and then walk away. You have to live with your spouse day in and day out. Truth isn't our enemy, and neither is our spouse. A reality check that draws us closer to God may be a spouse's loving gift.

Beaming Out into the World

By sharing time with others, telling them of God's plan for marriage, letting them see marital joy, and providing an example of positive behavior, Christians shine light into lives darkened by Satan's lies. God's truth begins in the home, with our own families, and beams out into the world.

Day 274

Expressions of Love

Thank You, Lord, for showing us how to love one another. This day, fill our hearts with ways to express that love.

Overcoming

Overcoming the world isn't a piece of cake. It takes great effort to do the right thing when the wrong is so tempting. Doing God's will, when the world says it's silly, challenges us. Those struggles we go through aren't meaningless, though they may seem so at the time. They're really indicators of overcoming. Are both of you overcoming today?

The Right Timing

God's time is not your time, and He can see much farther down the road than you can. Be patient while you're waiting for Him to work. Whether you're trying to make ends meet or struggling with your spouse, trust that the Lord is waiting to intervene when the moment is right. Remember that God is bound by His own promise to take care of you and your home, and God keeps His promises.

GALE HYATT

An Added Bonus

Use the gifts God has given you. In doing so, you will find your life blessed and, at the same time, be a blessing to others. And, as an added bonus, you'll be giving a gift to God. Is there anything better than that?

DONNA MALTESE

Blessed. . .Together!

Where is your focus? On your spouse's failings and shortcomings? Or on the One who can change each of us within and without? Count the blessings in your marriage. Thank God for the strengths of your marriage partner. He has done glorious things in bringing you together, keeping you together, and blessing you together.

MARGIE VAWTER

He's Love

Riches take wings, comforts vanish, hope withers away, but love stays with us. God is love.

LEW WALLACE

Loving Completely

Love, God's way, is the exact opposite of the worldly standard that demands perfection. God's love is offered first, before any action is done to earn it. That is how we are to be in our marriages. We offer love, unconditionally, to our spouses regardless of their actions or whether we deem them worthy. Loving our spouses in the way that God loves us means loving first, loving completely, and loving without condition.

NICOLE O'DELL

What God Sees

Lord, when we begin to worry too much about our outward appearance, remind us that others see You in us, and help us reflect that beauty in our lives.

Day 282

No "Nos"

There are no "nos" in God's promises. He never denies something He has said He will do or fails to follow through on a pledge He has made. Totally faithful to the words He has spoken, He comes through in the darkest moment or on the sunniest of days.

Anxiety Cure

Need a cure for anxiety? Rejoice in God, knowing He is near you. How can you worry when the Lord of the universe is at your side?

Day 284

Rejoice!

Rejoice in the Lord always. Again I will say, rejoice! . . . The Lord is at hand.

PHILIPPIANS 4:4–5 NKJV

Serving

Lord, we want to serve You, not gain kudos for ourselves. Whether it's a formal ministry or just the witness of our lives, let our actions glorify You.

Day 286

What Direction?

Discuss the path you are on as a couple. Do you need to turn around and go in another direction, walk more closely with God, or stay in your current direction? Do you need to make a turn that you've avoided so far?

A Wonderful Life

Truth lives in you through Jesus, not just today but forever. You can't evade truth, and why should you? Being close to Jesus and knowing how He wants you to live gives you a wonderful life.

Doubled Joy

This holy vow that man can make,
The golden thread in life,
The bond that none may dare to break,
That bindeth man and wife,
Which, blest by Thee, whate'er betide,
No evil shall destroy,
Through careworn days each care divides
And doubles every joy.

ADELAIDE THRUPP

Day 289

Represent Him

Whatever you do or say, represent Jesus well. May He be your focus so that others will be drawn to Him. Allow Jesus access to every part of your life, every day of your life. Don't hide your light under a bushel. Let it shine brightly to a world that is lost. May the light of Christ in you be clearly seen by others. Christ in you is indeed the hope of glory!

JULIE RAYBURN

Speak Gently

Gentle speech contributes to good communication, while frequent anger, voiced in loud tones, destroys a relationship. People can't hear what we say when we raise our voices and become nasty. All they recognize is the negative emotion behind the words—and they flee from it. Are we speaking gently today?

PAMELA MCQUADE

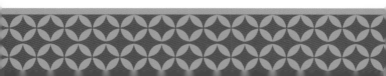

Always Right

If the words "I'm sorry" have a bad habit of getting stuck in your throat, it's time to ask the Lord for help. Listen to the still, small voice of your conscience. The Spirit of God will be faithful to let you know when an apology is in order. Obey that Voice and you'll always be right.

GALE HYATT

Day 292

Eye to Eye

Dear Father, I realize that my spouse and I will not always see eye to eye. Help me to admit fault when it is mine, to apologize when necessary, and to always be willing to change for the good of my marriage. Amen.

GALE HYATT

Unmatched Joy

Whenever we feel our hearts tighten over outcomes we want, we simply need to loosen our grip and take rest in God. This faith feels awkward at first in a world of independence and self-sufficiency, until we experience a joy unmatched by anything we can conjure up on our own. It is in these divine moments we can throw open the cupboard doors of our hearts and give away everything that's there, knowing that tomorrow we will be full again.

SARAH HAWKINS

Day 294

Our First Love

Even though God designed marriage for oneness, God still wants and needs to be our first love. God has to come before anything else in our lives. . .even before our spouse and kids. God is good and we can take refuge in Him anytime. He should be our main source of help, comfort, and security.

MARILEE PARRISH

Working It Out

Lord, when things go sour in our relationship, give us the patience and determination we need to hang in there and work things out between us with Your help.

Day 296

Rebuilt

A successful marriage is an edifice that must be rebuilt every day.

ANDRÉ MAUROIS

Something More Worthwhile

We can overcome evil with good. We can stand our ground, smile politely, and treat our enemies with love and consideration. If we keep it up, they'll either leave us alone or begin to change their minds about us. Let's give them something more worthwhile to think about.

Day 298

Been There, Done That

Why go around and around in the same circle when your elders have already done that lap and can show you a shortcut? Today, information is readily available on almost any subject—more information than we can ever process ourselves. We need to know what information is useful and profitable and what is just junk. Ask those who have already been there, done that.

Financial Wisdom

No one plans on poverty and want. People don't set them as life goals. But the daily elements of work and good budget management that keep us going financially keep them at bay. Is God managing your life—or are you?

A Blossoming Relationship

Every day, we need to live in truth, putting off that old, sinful self. As truth grows in our lives, our marriage relationship can blossom, too.

PAMELA MCQUADE

Uniquely Created

It's no secret that God created us uniquely. That's part of what keeps marriage so fun and interesting, but we must all do our parts. Yes, your spouse has a role to fill, but it's God's job to see that he or she does it.

RACHEL QUILLIN

God's Word on Husbands and Wives

The wife hath not power of her own body, but the husband: and likewise also the husband hath not power of his own body, but the wife.

1 CORINTHIANS 7:4 KJV

Anger Management

Dear God, help me to be loving and forgiving even when I am angry with my spouse. Teach me to control my feelings and to handle my anger in a way that pleases You. Amen.

GALE HYATT

No Matter What

Each time we feel we can't bear up under the hurt, we must remember the times and ways we have hurt God. How does He react? Does He lash out in anger? Does He turn His back on us and refuse to acknowledge our presence? Never. God is always there with His arms outstretched, love shining from Him like a beacon to our wounded souls. We need to learn to be likewise to our spouses, no matter what.

NANCY FARRIER

Closer

Present your needs and requests to God. He will respond by supplying strength and power. His grace will be sufficient to meet every need you encounter. When you rely upon the Lord, even your attitude will change. Instead of harboring bitterness and anger, rejoice in the Lord's provision! Your relationship with the Lord and your [spouse] will grow closer.

JULIE RAYBURN

Standing By

To love means to communicate to the other, that you will never fail him or let him down when he needs you, but that you will always be standing by with all the necessary encouragements. It is something one can communicate to another only if one has it.

ASHLEY MONTAGU

Nearer to God—and to Each Other

When, as couples, we share our lives with our Lord though joint Bible study and prayer, not only do we draw near Him; we draw near to each other. Then we love God with all our hearts and souls and begin to fulfill His will for our marriages, too.

PAMELA MCQUADE

Drawn to You

Father, I want my marriage to be a reflection of Your grace, Your goodness, Your righteousness. May others be drawn to You through our marriage. Amen.

MARGIE VAWTER

Marriage Covenant

The marriage covenant we entered into, the vows we exchanged, and even many of the traditions we observed on our wedding day are a picture of the covenant relationship God desires to have with us in Jesus Christ. When we enter into marriage, God calls us to demonstrate His righteousness, love, and grace to others. Knowing we are imperfect examples, He guards and supports us so His love and righteousness shine through our marriages.

MARGIE VAWTER

Day 310

Closely Connected

As a Christian, you are part of God's church—His beloved. You are His, and He is yours. Just as you closely identify with your spouse, God identifies with you. He connects closely with those whom He loves.

He Knows You Intimately

God knows you, your day-to-day issues, and the works you do for Him. He joined you and your spouse together in marriage and knows each of you intimately. Every detail of your lives is open to Him.

Day 312

Walk in Truth

We can't re-create God in our own image and be happy. Wrong doctrine takes all the power out of faith and destroys God's ability to work in our lives. Instead of falling for a bunch of maybes, be renewed in the knowledge of God by believing just what He said about His plan for salvation and walking in that truth. Then you'll be blessed with a new you, no maybes about it.

The Meaning of Love

Love does not mean one thing in man and another thing in God. . . . The divine heart is human in its sympathies.

FREDERICK WILLIAM ROBERTSON

Day 314

Blessings at Work

Lord Jesus, we know Your blessings are at work in our lives. Keep us faithful when we can't see them.

God's Spirit

Don't let lack of forgiveness damage your life and relationships. Instead, let God's Spirit use your life in His work.

Day 316

Refuge

God hasn't stopped blessing you when troubles come. He becomes your blessing—He's there for you when you hurt, and your protector from harm.

Transparent

Allow yourself to become transparent to God and to your spouse. Ask God to "show me" to me. When we allow Him to expose the truth of who we are, He brings everything to the light. When we are reproved by His love, then our weaknesses are made visible and He is able to heal the past wounds and hurts that have controlled our behavior and speech.

SHANNA GREGOR

DAY 318

Alive and Well

If you are fortunate enough to love and be loved, consider yourself blessed indeed. Cherish that love. Nurture it. Go out of your way to protect it. Like so many worthy things, love isn't easy. But when the tale of your years has been told, you'll be glad you kept it alive and well.

GALE HYATT

For Each Other

Selfishness is one of those marriage stresses that will never heal on its own because it can never be fulfilled. Selfishness is never satisfied. Rather than selfish pursuits, begin to live for each other, share in decisions—be the partners that God created you to be.

NICOLE O'DELL

Marital Partnership

In marriage, like any real partnership, there is no room for selfishness or single-minded agendas. Each spouse should look for ways to build each other up for the good of the marriage and work together to identify and accomplish goals. When we work with our spouse as a partner, we are helping the marriage become all that God intended it to be.

NICOLE O'DELL

Things That Truly Matter

While it doesn't ensure perfection, setting aside a short time each morning to focus on the Father and the day ahead can help prepare us to live more intentionally. In this time, like Jesus, we gain clarity so that we can invest our lives in the things that will truly matter.

JOANNA BLOSS

Day 322

Precious in God's Sight

God sees each time we sacrifice our own wants and needs to help our spouse. He knows, even if no one else does. We can rest in that, not allowing our pride to dictate how we should be treated. Let us consider our mate, and see how precious he or she is in God's sight.

NANCY FARRIER

His Glory

Humble yourself before the Lord and He will lift you up. He will shine through you. You will reflect and make known His glory. May it be so!

JULIE RAYBURN

Day 324

A Blessed Year

How has God blessed you through the year? Have you faced some unusual trials or struggles? Or has life been unusually smooth? What do you have to praise Him for?

Indescribable

Thanks be to God for his indescribable gift!

2 CORINTHIANS 9:15 NIV

Day 326

Living Presents

Even if we can't spend a fortune on gifts at Christmastime, we can act like Jesus and become living presents who give our lives to those we love. We, too, can become indescribable gifts who touch the lives of needy, hurting souls.

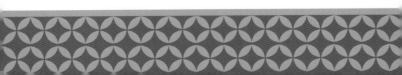

To Love

To love is to place our happiness
in the happiness of another.

GOTTFRIED WILHELM VON LEIBNIZ

Day 328

Tomorrow

Lord, we want to praise You today for Your plans for tomorrow. Help us trust in You before we see every outcome.

The Good News

Have you told others that God offers them peace, good things, and salvation? Or has your mouth been closed by fear? Don't let the year pass without offering the good news to someone. Pray about reaching out, and God will show you a need. All you have to do is respond.

Day 330

Control

We can try to control our lives in many ways: spiritually, financially, organizationally, and so on. We certainly need to have some sense of where we are and where we're going. Are there some control issues hanging over your life? Together, try to identify them. Are they based on a lack of control or too much?

Relationship Repair

Relationships wax and wane, but God doesn't. He always loves both of you. Together you can come before Him and engage in relationship repair. The emotional space that seems eternal doesn't need to be.

PAMELA MCQUADE

The Other Side

Listening to the other side of an argument can be enlightening if we'll give the other person a chance; speaking calmly, without anger, will lead to much more constructive conversations which will, in turn, build healthier marriages and relationships.

MANDY NYDEGGER

Honoring Your Mate

Our selfish desires cause us to fight and rebel against what we have rather than accept and appreciate our blessings. Constant comparison with other marriages, spouses, families, will only lead to disappointment and regret. Instead, focus on the life that God speaks into your marriage when He reveals the gifts He has given to you through the blessing of your spouse.

NICOLE O'DELL

R-E-S-P-E-C-T

Respect involves submission, humility, and appreciation. Mistakenly, many couples believe these things need to be earned, even in marriage. That is true with conditional love, but God's design for marriage is based upon unconditional love for each other. Respectful ways are a natural part of unconditional love. Respect, in a Christian marriage, isn't offered as a reward; it's given as a gift.

NICOLE O'DELL

Properly Balanced

It is the law of supply and demand—the more love you give, the more love you will have to give. Soon it will be overflowing, and yours will be a joyful home.

RACHEL QUILLIN

More Than Enough

With Jesus in our lives, we dare not look at what we lack—in our marriage, our family, our job, or church. Instead, He wants us to take what we have and give it to Him. By doing so, He will bless our meager store and multiply it. And in the end, we will find we have more than enough!

DONNA MALTESE

Warm for a Lifetime

In order to nurture romance, we need to realize that it's a verb, it requires action, and it's a priority. Appreciate your spouse and show gratitude; learn new things about each other. Give your spouse your time, your attention, your affection, and your respect, knowing that when you give, you will receive the rewards of romance. Romance is a flame which, if properly tended, will keep you warm for a lifetime.

NICOLE O'DELL

Day 338

Passions

Love is of all passions the strongest, for it attacks simultaneously the head, the heart, and the senses.

VOLTAIRE

The Answer to Every Need

Jesus, the gift straight from God, reaches places in the soul no human goes. Small and pitiable on the outside on the night of His birth, inside He still held all the answers to every human need. We need never be ruled by anyone else.

Day 340

Wisdom from God

Even the wisest human beings cannot know everything. Extremely discerning folks still make mistakes because they don't have enough information. The only wisdom that never fails is from God.

Not Finished

Just as God looked after Jesus, He also looks after you.
He has created you for a purpose in this world and will
see that purpose through to completion.
So when money is short, you face a dozen challenges,
or relationships seem stressed,
remember God is not finished.

Day 342

Places of Action

In marriage, God sometimes calls us out of protected places into places of action. They may not be comfortable, and they aren't often the places we thought we'd be in. Staying in our nice, comfy spots seems more desirable. But obedience to God requires that we answer the uncomfortable call.

For All People

As you face a new year, are you confident God will keep His promises? When God makes them, it's not just in the abstract. He means His promises for people—all of us who believe in Him.

Day 344

Every Promise

Thank You, God, for Your faithfulness to every promise. We can trust in You.

Great Gain

Sometimes we believe we know what God wants for us, only to have Him lead us in a different direction. This could mean a move, or a new job, maybe even a change in lifestyle because our income decreases. No matter what the direction is, we need to be content to follow God wherever He sends us. When we are willing to do this, we will be blessed with godliness and rewarded with great gain.

NANCY FARRIER

Day 346

As God Planned

Today why don't you challenge yourself anew to love your spouse the way God planned? Determine to cherish him or her for better or for worse. You might be amazed at what it will do for your marriage and family.

RACHEL QUILLIN

Most Important

Most important of all, continue to show deep love for each other, for love covers a multitude of sins.

1 PETER 4:8 NLT

Whole

Love is like a tranquil breeze that sweeps over my soul, making me whole.

UNKNOWN

A Common Goal

When we experience differences with our spouses, and when arguments become common, the answer is not to distance ourselves or walk away. Instead, we are to love each other. God says that love covers over sins. Love allows us to forgive, to merge our differences into a common goal, and to accomplish that goal together with support and encouragement.

MANDY NYDEGGER

Day 350

Follow the Leader

Jesus is our leader. It's imperative that we keep our eyes on Him for direction and instruction. How else will we be able to navigate wisely in the world? He will communicate His will for our lives day by day. He will make our paths straight and show us the way to go. Let's keep our eyes on Jesus so we can follow our leader!

JULIE RAYBURN

Know Him Better

Father God, we don't often appreciate Your beauty, splendor, strength, and majesty. Forgive us for our shallowness. We want to know You better.

A Light Burden

As we learn to rest in God's love, we realize that His yoke—the "burden" of love—is easy. And as we learn to express our love in acts of service, the burden of responsibility begins to lift.

MARGIE VAWTER

Teachable Hearts

Having a teachable heart is a gift from God. We must pray that He will help us see the changes we need to make. Instead of defending our actions with poor reactions, let us take a step back and pray that God will teach us what we need to know.

NANCY FARRIER

Christmas Every Day

As you limber up the credit cards at Christmastime
to provide the gifts your children request, remind
yourself that your heavenly Father, the perfect parent,
goes Christmas shopping every day of the year for you,
answering your prayers, seeing to your needs,
and doing it all out of His perfect love for you.

Love as He Loves

It is hard to avoid the clarity of Jesus' message: Love people to the extent which He loves (John 13:34). Since God is the creator of love, He is the standard by which we are measured. He loves sacrificially, completely, and passionately without keeping a record of past failures. Can we love our spouses like that?

SARAH HAWKINS

Day 356

How Delightful

How delightful is your love. . . . How much more pleasing is your love than wine, and the fragrance of your perfume than any spice!

SONG OF SONGS 4:10 NIV

Christ's Ambassadors

Although Christians are far from perfect, we are called to be Christ's ambassadors, His representatives. In a world filled with darkness, we have the privilege of being light to those that are lost. By reflecting His glory, we proclaim His truth: Jesus Christ is the way, the truth, and the life.

JULIE RAYBURN

Day 358

Take On the World

God joins two people together in the covenant bond of marriage because they complete each other with their strengths and gifts. When not partnered together, those two people are only working with half of the strengths that God has given them. Rather than battling and fighting against partnership, why not join with your spouse as one unit, together with God, to take on the world together?

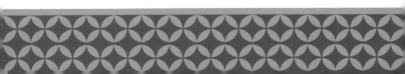

NICOLE O'DELL

Pass It Down

Families often record facts about their history. But a couple also can pass down a few special cards or notes that encourage the next generation's marriages with love, faithfulness, and fun.

RACHAEL PHILLIPS

Day 360

Cling

Lord of love, the world wages war against our marriage. Please help us cling to You and each other, celebrating every victory we can. Amen.

RACHAEL PHILLIPS

Day 361

No Silent Treatment

Stuffing our feelings doesn't make them go away. Instead, it makes them build up and simmer to a slow boil, eventually causing us to explode in anger, saying things we later regret. While it's not realistic or beneficial to say everything that pops into our heads, it is a wise practice to share feelings as they arise. Both your marriage and your emotional health will benefit when you share your feelings in an honest and loving way.

JOANNA BLOSS

Love Is. . .

Love is the glue that holds a marriage together. It is the bond that will last for better or worse, for richer or poorer, in sickness and in health. Love will overlook faults and forgive offenses rather than seek revenge. It is understanding, kind, and easy to please. Love doesn't sulk or pout. It isn't selfish or calculating. It is fierce yet gentle, powerful yet meek. It is the single ingredient that will hold your marriage together long after beauty has faded and health has declined.

GALE HYATT

All Our Days

Satisfy us in the morning. . .that we may sing for joy and be glad all our days. . . . May the favor of the Lord our God rest upon us; establish the work of our hands.

PSALM 90:14, 17 NIV

For Life

Dear Father, thank You for giving me someone to love. Help me to do everything within my power to keep my love for my spouse strong, so that our marriage will last for as long as we both shall live. Amen.

GALE HYATT

Seeing You

Father, we thank You for all the blessings You have given us. May we live our lives in such a way that others will see You in our lives and believe.

Notes